This Pet Journal Belongs To:

MY PET Profile

NAME: COAT COLOR:

BREED: EYE COLOR:

BIRTHDAY: SPECIAL MARKINGS:

GENDER: MEDICAL CONDITIONS:

ID CHIP #:   WEIGHT :

ALLERGIES: FAVORITE TOYS:

            SPAY/NEUTERED: YES: NO:

NOTES:

Vet Information

NAME/BUSINESS:

PHONE:

EMAIL:

ADDRESS:

Groomer Information

NAME/BUSINESS:

PHONE:

EMAIL:

ADDRESS:

PET *Vaccination Chart*

YEAR:

PET NAME:		DOB:	GENDER:

VACCINATION HISTORY

DATE:	VACCINATION:	AGE:	NOTES:

VETERINARY CARE *Tracker*

DATE:　　　　**DESCRIPTION:**　　　　**LOCATION:**　　　　**AMOUNT:**

PET HEALTH
Immunization Records

DATE:	AGE:	TYPE:	GIVEN BY:	NEXT DUE:

PET HEALTH
Medication Records

DATE:	AGE:	MEDICATION:	GIVEN BY:	NEXT DUE:

PET MEDICATION *Tracker*

DATE & TIME:	MEDICATION:	FREQUENCY:	DOSAGE:

PET WELLNESS *Journal*

YEAR:

PET NAME: DOB: GENDER:

WELLNESS HISTORY

DATE:	DESCRIPTION:	TREATMENT:	NOTES:

PET SITTER *Notes*
- RESPONSIBILITIES -

	M	T	W	T	F	S	S

MY PET Expenses

MONTH: **YEAR:**

PET NAME:

EXPENSE TRACKER

DATE	FOOD	VET	MEDICATION	GROOMING	COST
					$
					$
					$
					$
					$
					$
					$
					$
					$
					$
					$
					$
					$
					$
					$

MY PET Expenses

MONTH: YEAR:

PET NAME:

EXPENSE TRACKER

DATE	FOOD	VET	MEDICATION	GROOMING	COST
					$
					$
					$
					$
					$
					$
					$
					$
					$
					$
					$
					$
					$
					$
					$

MONTHLY PET *Overview*

JANUARY   **FEBRUARY**   **MARCH**

APRIL   **MAY**   **JUNE**

MONTHLY PET *Overview*

JULY	AUGUST	SEPTEMBER

OCTOBER	NOVEMBER	DECEMBER

WEEKLY PET *Journal*

WEEK OF: ....

MONDAY   **TUESDAY**   **WEDNESDAY**

THURSDAY   **FRIDAY**   **SATURDAY**

SUNDAY   **WEEKLY NOTES**

MY PET Journal

_____

_____
_____
_____
_____
_____
_____
_____
_____
_____
_____
_____
_____
_____
_____
_____
_____
_____
_____
_____
_____

WEEKLY PET *Journal*

MONDAY

TUESDAY

WEDNESDAY

THURSDAY

FRIDAY

SATURDAY

SUNDAY

WEEKLY NOTES

MY PET *Journal*

WEEK OF

WEEKLY PET *Journal*

WEEK OF: ....

MONDAY

TUESDAY

WEDNESDAY

THURSDAY

FRIDAY

SATURDAY

SUNDAY

WEEKLY NOTES

MY PET Journal

_____
_____
_____
_____
_____
_____
_____
_____
_____
_____
_____
_____
_____
_____
_____
_____
_____
_____
_____
_____
_____
_____
_____
_____
_____

WEEKLY PET *Journal*

WEEK OF: _____

MONDAY

TUESDAY

WEDNESDAY

THURSDAY

FRIDAY

SATURDAY

SUNDAY

WEEKLY NOTES

MY PET Journal

WEEK OF:

WEEKLY PET *Journal*

WEEK OF: _____

MONDAY

TUESDAY

WEDNESDAY

THURSDAY

FRIDAY

SATURDAY

SUNDAY

WEEKLY NOTES

MY PET Journal

_____
_____
_____
_____
_____
_____
_____
_____
_____
_____
_____
_____
_____
_____
_____
_____
_____
_____
_____
_____
_____

WEEKLY PET *Journal*

WEEK OF: _____

MONDAY   **TUESDAY**   **WEDNESDAY**

THURSDAY   **FRIDAY**   **SATURDAY**

SUNDAY   **WEEKLY NOTES**

MY PET Journal

WEEK OF

MONDAY   TUESDAY   WEDNESDAY

WEEKLY PET *Journal*

WEEK OF: ....

MONDAY

TUESDAY

WEDNESDAY

THURSDAY

FRIDAY

SATURDAY

SUNDAY

WEEKLY NOTES

MY PET Journal

_____

_____

_____

_____

_____

_____

_____

_____

_____

_____

_____

_____

_____

_____

_____

_____

_____

_____

_____

_____

_____

WEEKLY PET *Journal*

WEEK OF: ....

MONDAY

TUESDAY

WEDNESDAY

THURSDAY

FRIDAY

SATURDAY

SUNDAY

WEEKLY NOTES

MY PET Journal

WEEK OF:

MONDAY   TUESDAY   WEDNESDAY

WEEKLY PET *Journal*

MONDAY

TUESDAY

WEDNESDAY

THURSDAY

FRIDAY

SATURDAY

SUNDAY

WEEKLY NOTES

MY PET Journal

_____
_____
_____
_____
_____
_____
_____
_____
_____
_____
_____
_____
_____
_____
_____
_____
_____
_____
_____
_____
_____
_____
_____

WEEKLY PET *Journal*

WEEK OF: _____

MONDAY

TUESDAY

WEDNESDAY

THURSDAY

FRIDAY

SATURDAY

SUNDAY

WEEKLY NOTES

MY PET Journal

WEEK OF

WEDNESDAY   TUESDAY   MONDAY

WEEKLY PET *Journal*

WEEK OF: ....

MONDAY	TUESDAY	WEDNESDAY

THURSDAY	FRIDAY	SATURDAY

SUNDAY

WEEKLY NOTES

MY PET Journal

WEEKLY PET *Journal*

WEEK OF: _____

MONDAY

TUESDAY

WEDNESDAY

THURSDAY

FRIDAY

SATURDAY

SUNDAY

WEEKLY NOTES

MY PET Journal

WEEKLY PET *Journal*

MONDAY

TUESDAY

WEDNESDAY

THURSDAY

FRIDAY

SATURDAY

SUNDAY

WEEKLY NOTES

MY PET Journal

WEEKLY PET *Journal*

WEEK OF: _____

MONDAY

TUESDAY

WEDNESDAY

THURSDAY

FRIDAY

SATURDAY

SUNDAY

WEEKLY NOTES

MY PET Journal

WEEK OF

MONDAY   TUESDAY   WEDNESDAY

WEEKLY PET *Journal*

WEEK OF: _____

MONDAY

TUESDAY

WEDNESDAY

THURSDAY

FRIDAY

SATURDAY

SUNDAY

WEEKLY NOTES

MY PET Journal

WEEKLY PET *Journal*

WEEK OF: _____

MONDAY

TUESDAY

WEDNESDAY

THURSDAY

FRIDAY

SATURDAY

SUNDAY

WEEKLY NOTES

MY PET Journal

WEEKLY PET *Journal*

MONDAY

TUESDAY

WEDNESDAY

THURSDAY

FRIDAY

SATURDAY

SUNDAY

WEEKLY NOTES

MY PET Journal

WEEKLY PET *Journal*

WEEK OF: _____

MONDAY

TUESDAY

WEDNESDAY

THURSDAY

FRIDAY

SATURDAY

SUNDAY

WEEKLY NOTES

MY PET Journal

WEEK OF

MONDAY   TUESDAY   WEDNESDAY

WEEKLY PET *Journal*

WEEK OF: ....

MONDAY

TUESDAY

WEDNESDAY

THURSDAY

FRIDAY

SATURDAY

SUNDAY

WEEKLY NOTES

MY PET Journal

_____

_____

_____

_____

_____

_____

_____

_____

_____

_____

_____

_____

_____

_____

_____

_____

_____

_____

_____

WEEKLY PET *Journal*

WEEK OF: _____

MONDAY   TUESDAY   WEDNESDAY

THURSDAY   FRIDAY   SATURDAY

SUNDAY   WEEKLY NOTES

MY PET Journal

WEEKLY PET *Journal*

WEEK OF: ....

MONDAY

TUESDAY

WEDNESDAY

THURSDAY

FRIDAY

SATURDAY

SUNDAY

WEEKLY NOTES

MY PET Journal

_____

_____
_____
_____
_____
_____
_____
_____
_____
_____
_____
_____
_____
_____
_____
_____
_____
_____
_____
_____
_____
_____

WEEKLY PET *Journal*

WEEK OF: _____

MONDAY   **TUESDAY**   **WEDNESDAY**

THURSDAY   **FRIDAY**   **SATURDAY**

SUNDAY   **WEEKLY NOTES**

MY PET Journal

WEEK OF:

WEDNESDAY   TUESDAY   MONDAY

WEEKLY PET *Journal*

WEEK OF: _____

MONDAY

TUESDAY

WEDNESDAY

THURSDAY

FRIDAY

SATURDAY

SUNDAY

WEEKLY NOTES

MY PET Journal

WEEKLY PET *Journal*

WEEK OF: _____

MONDAY   **TUESDAY**   **WEDNESDAY**

THURSDAY   **FRIDAY**   **SATURDAY**

SUNDAY   **WEEKLY NOTES**

MY PET Journal

WEEKLY PET *Journal*

WEEK OF: _____

MONDAY

TUESDAY

WEDNESDAY

THURSDAY

FRIDAY

SATURDAY

SUNDAY

WEEKLY NOTES

MY PET Journal

WEEKLY PET *Journal*

WEEK OF: ....

MONDAY

TUESDAY

WEDNESDAY

THURSDAY

FRIDAY

SATURDAY

SUNDAY

WEEKLY NOTES

MY PET Journal

WEEK OF

MONDAY   TUESDAY   WEDNESDAY

WEEKLY PET *Journal*

WEEK OF: ....

MONDAY

TUESDAY

WEDNESDAY

THURSDAY

FRIDAY

SATURDAY

SUNDAY

WEEKLY NOTES

MY PET *Journal*

WEEKLY PET *Journal*

WEEK OF: ....

MONDAY

TUESDAY

WEDNESDAY

THURSDAY

FRIDAY

SATURDAY

SUNDAY

WEEKLY NOTES

MY PET Journal

WEEKLY PET *Journal*

WEEK OF: _____

MONDAY

TUESDAY

WEDNESDAY

THURSDAY

FRIDAY

SATURDAY

SUNDAY

WEEKLY NOTES

MY PET Journal

WEEKLY PET *Journal*

WEEK OF: ....

MONDAY

TUESDAY

WEDNESDAY

THURSDAY

FRIDAY

SATURDAY

SUNDAY

WEEKLY NOTES

MY PET Journal

WEEK OF

WEDNESDAY   TUESDAY   MONDAY

WEEKLY PET *Journal*

WEEK OF: _____

MONDAY

TUESDAY

WEDNESDAY

THURSDAY

FRIDAY

SATURDAY

SUNDAY

WEEKLY NOTES

MY PET Journal

WEEKLY PET *Journal*

WEEK OF: _____

MONDAY

TUESDAY

WEDNESDAY

THURSDAY

FRIDAY

SATURDAY

SUNDAY

WEEKLY NOTES

MY PET Journal

WEEK OF:

MONDAY   TUESDAY   WEDNESDAY

WEEKLY PET *Journal*

WEEK OF: ....

MONDAY

TUESDAY

WEDNESDAY

THURSDAY

FRIDAY

SATURDAY

SUNDAY

WEEKLY NOTES

MY PET Journal

(lined writing area)

(two empty boxes at the bottom of the page)

WEEKLY PET *Journal*

WEEK OF: _____

MONDAY

TUESDAY

WEDNESDAY

THURSDAY

FRIDAY

SATURDAY

SUNDAY

WEEKLY NOTES

MY PET Journal

WEEK OF
WEDNESDAY TUESDAY MONDA

WEEKLY PET *Journal*

MONDAY

TUESDAY

WEDNESDAY

THURSDAY

FRIDAY

SATURDAY

SUNDAY

WEEKLY NOTES

MY PET Journal

(lined writing area)

WEEKLY PET *Journal*

WEEK OF: _____

MONDAY

TUESDAY

WEDNESDAY

THURSDAY

FRIDAY

SATURDAY

SUNDAY

WEEKLY NOTES

MY PET Journal

WEEK OF:

MONDAY   TUESDAY   WEDNESDAY

WEEKLY PET *Journal*

WEEK OF: _____

MONDAY

TUESDAY

WEDNESDAY

THURSDAY

FRIDAY

SATURDAY

SUNDAY

WEEKLY NOTES

MY PET Journal

WEEKLY PET *Journal*

WEEK OF: _____

MONDAY

TUESDAY

WEDNESDAY

THURSDAY

FRIDAY

SATURDAY

SUNDAY

WEEKLY NOTES

MY PET Journal

WEEK OF

MONDAY   TUESDAY   WEDNESDAY

WEEKLY PET *Journal*

WEEK OF: ....

MONDAY

TUESDAY

WEDNESDAY

THURSDAY

FRIDAY

SATURDAY

SUNDAY

WEEKLY NOTES

MY PET Journal

_____
_____
_____
_____
_____
_____
_____
_____
_____
_____
_____
_____
_____
_____
_____
_____
_____
_____
_____
_____
_____

WEEKLY PET *Journal*

WEEK OF: ....

MONDAY

TUESDAY

WEDNESDAY

THURSDAY

FRIDAY

SATURDAY

SUNDAY

WEEKLY NOTES

MY PET Journal

WEEK OF

WEDNESDAY · TUESDAY · MONDAY

WEEKLY PET Journal

WEEK OF: _____

MONDAY

TUESDAY

WEDNESDAY

THURSDAY

FRIDAY

SATURDAY

SUNDAY

WEEKLY NOTES

MY PET Journal

_____
_____
_____
_____
_____
_____
_____
_____
_____
_____
_____
_____
_____
_____
_____
_____
_____
_____
_____
_____
_____
_____
_____
_____

WEEKLY PET *Journal*

WEEK OF: _____

MONDAY

TUESDAY

WEDNESDAY

THURSDAY

FRIDAY

SATURDAY

SUNDAY

WEEKLY NOTES

MY PET Journal

(lined writing space with two boxes at the bottom)

WEEKLY PET *Journal*

WEEK OF: _____

MONDAY

TUESDAY

WEDNESDAY

THURSDAY

FRIDAY

SATURDAY

SUNDAY

WEEKLY NOTES

MY PET Journal

WEEK OF

SUNDAY   MONDAY

WEDNESDAY

WEEKLY PET *Journal*

WEEK OF: ....

MONDAY

TUESDAY

WEDNESDAY

THURSDAY

FRIDAY

SATURDAY

SUNDAY

WEEKLY NOTES

MY PET Journal

WEEKLY PET *Journal*

WEEK OF: ....

MONDAY

TUESDAY

WEDNESDAY

THURSDAY

FRIDAY

SATURDAY

SUNDAY

WEEKLY NOTES

MY PET Journal

_____
_____
_____
_____
_____
_____
_____
_____
_____
_____
_____
_____
_____
_____
_____
_____
_____
_____
_____
_____
_____
_____
_____
_____

WEEKLY PET *Journal*

WEEK OF: ....

MONDAY

TUESDAY

WEDNESDAY

THURSDAY

FRIDAY

SATURDAY

SUNDAY

WEEKLY NOTES

MY PET *Journal*

WEEK OF:

MONDAY   TUESDAY   WEDNESDAY

WEEKLY PET *Journal*

WEEK OF: ....

MONDAY

TUESDAY

WEDNESDAY

THURSDAY

FRIDAY

SATURDAY

SUNDAY

WEEKLY NOTES

MY PET Journal

(blank lined journal page with two empty boxes at the bottom)

WEEKLY PET *Journal*

WEEK OF: ....

MONDAY

TUESDAY

WEDNESDAY

THURSDAY

FRIDAY

SATURDAY

SUNDAY

WEEKLY NOTES

MY PET Journal

WEEKLY PET *Journal*

WEEK OF: ....

MONDAY

TUESDAY

WEDNESDAY

THURSDAY

FRIDAY

SATURDAY

SUNDAY

WEEKLY NOTES

MY PET *Journal*

WEEKLY PET *Journal*

WEEK OF: _____

MONDAY

TUESDAY

WEDNESDAY

THURSDAY

FRIDAY

SATURDAY

SUNDAY

WEEKLY NOTES

MY PET Journal

WEEK OF

MONDAY   TUESDAY   WEDNESDAY

WEEKLY PET *Journal*

WEEK OF: _____

MONDAY

TUESDAY

WEDNESDAY

THURSDAY

FRIDAY

SATURDAY

SUNDAY

WEEKLY NOTES

MY PET Journal

(lined writing area)

(two empty boxes at the bottom)

WEEKLY PET *Journal*

WEEK OF: ....

MONDAY

TUESDAY

WEDNESDAY

THURSDAY

FRIDAY

SATURDAY

SUNDAY

WEEKLY NOTES

MY PET Journal

WEEK OF

MONDAY   TUESDAY   WEDNESDAY

MY PET *Journal*

MY PET Journal

_____
_____
_____
_____
_____
_____
_____
_____
_____
_____
_____
_____
_____
_____
_____
_____
_____
_____
_____
_____
_____
_____
_____